## PRAISE

The poems in *Blood on Blood* are both fan fiction & testament. Devin Kelly vividly sketches out the lives of characters from Bruce Springsteen's Nebraska album. A serial killer is decked out in "a suit all paisley / & pink" & a girl "dips a French fry / in her coke." Kelly's images are bewitching & luminous. His phrasing captures the swerves & pauses of spoken speech. The poems also testify to the eternal-but-fleeting bonds between father & son & between brothers. In one poem, a speaker, remembering a car ride with his deceased father, says, "You are so much his you cannot contain / your love." Confession: I cried when I read those lines. Kelly's poems are full of small mercies & blood-warm insights. I highly recommend this book.
— **Eduardo C. Corral**, author, *Slow Lightning*

"Kelly goes between the songs, between the words, the notes. He keeps going until he hits marrow. This isn't tribute. It's the work we knew was inside Springsteen's masterpiece all along."
— **William Lessard**, author, *Rembrandt with Cell Phone*

"This is poetry to live with. Devin Kelly is an American writer who's spun life and song into a traveling tale of petty crime, of a blue kind of violence, of love at dusk and dawn, and of God (whoever she is). Kelly's is a world of meaning and unmasking, an astonishing poetry of loss and becoming."
— **A.M. Davenport,** editor of *Full Stop* and *The Scofield*

"Devin Kelly is a master storyteller. He weaves together mysterious lyricism with narrative so naturally and effectively, I feel like I know the narrator like myself, but am excitedly intrigued by the ghostly presence of all the characters. Each poem makes me want to know more, makes me hungry for details and more lines. Kelly takes surprising turns and twists while telling it like it is, such as in this line: "God's a good lie. & even God knows." He's definitely a poet to watch."
— **Joanna C. Valente**, author of, *The Gods Are Dead*

# BLOOD ON BLOOD

*A Reimagining of*
*Bruce Springsteen's*
*Nebraska*

## DEVIN KELLY

Copyright © 2016 by DEVIN KELLY

PUBLISHED BY UNKNOWN PRESS

First Edition

All rights reserved. Nothing may be reproduced without permission of the writer or publisher, unless the work is being quoted in short critical reviews or interviews.

Design by Rae Buleri and Bud Smith

Some of these poems first appeared in one form or another in the following journals:

*El Balazo Press*: "Middle America," & "At the End of Every Hard-Earned Day"; *ELKE*: "My Father's House"; FLAPPERHOUSE: "After Lincoln, Nebraska," & "Litany of What We Killed"; The Grief Diaries" "Mansion on the Hill"; *Hobart*: "Why I Might Coach the Little League Team"; *Ohio Edit*: "Franky Drives the Trans-Canada Highway & Stops at a Diner," & "My Father & I at a Denny's in Lansing"; Public Pool: "Aubade for a Nebraska Morning" & "Aubade for a Nebraska Night"; The Nervous Breakdown: "Nebraska"

*for my brother & the shit we did*

"Me & Franky laughing & drinking,
nothing feels better than blood on blood."

Bruce Springsteen, 'Highway Patrolman'

# CONTENTS

13
Middle America
After Lincoln, Nebraska
Litany of What We Killed
Why Women Make the Best Kind of Killers
The Story of How You & Your Brother Grew Up

23
Brothers in Town
Highway Patrolman
Watching Your Father Drive
Elegy for Maria & My Brother
My Father's House
The Story of How You & Your Brother Grew Up

37
Open All Night
Atlantic City
Franky Drives North on 385 Toward Chadron
Aubade for a Nebraska Morning
The Story of How You & Your Brother Grew Up

49  Why I Might Coach the Little League Team
    Golden Shovel from Atlantic City
    Franky Lingers at a Roy Rodgers
    Mahwah Assembly
    Confession
    The Story of How You & Your Brother Grew Up

63  Everybody Is Sick With the Flu
    How to Use Old Sparky
    Franky Drives the Trans-Canada Highway & Stops at a Diner
    Ice Fishing
    Aubade for a Nebraska Night
    The Story of How You & Your Brother Grew Up

    Poem for My Brother Running Around a Track
79  My Father & I At a Denny's in Lansing
    Franky Stops at a Payphone to Call His Brother Joey
    Up All Night
    Reason to Believe
    The Story of How You & Your Brother Grew Up

95  Nebraska
    Franky's Apology
    At the End of Every Hard-Earned Day
    While Waiting to See Bruce
    Mansion on the Hill

BLOOD ON BLOOD

## MIDDLE AMERICA

It began with a river & its crossing,
    a whisker of grain pulled out of a dead

boy's mouth, fur strung tight & propped
    with bone. A gunshot, a silence,

& another. Believe me when I say
    I was raised alright. You can

forgive a marriage for having a child
    but you cannot forgive its love.

It began with want & ended with more.
    I wanted to lower the horizon line

until it hovered before my toes, so that
    I might step into sky & be bluer

than a feeling. You can say it began
        with rib torn from body; you can

say clay; you can say dust. Who is it
        you want to excuse from evil?

I was taught love is patient & kind.
        In this, I was taught love, simple

& burning, exists. I am a fool. It began
        with my hand on objects. It ended

with the way an object can hold a soul,
        become a kind of body. Look around.

There is nothing here but the high fever
        of waving grass as far as eye can see.

There's no room for shadow. When I wanted
        to hide, I had to crawl inside my body.

## AFTER LINCOLN, NEBRASKA

Through the Badlands we killed
& made our killing into love.

That time I went, sawed-off,
through the back door while you

charmed the checkout clerk
for some bread. I want to say

love's real fun, but I don't know
what came first — that smile

you cheeked while I peeked down
your blouse to find the wad of bills

you robbed like the sunlight stolen
in your hair, or the kiss of your knee on

mine as we drove all night under
big moon & stars & some

good or evil god. We was something
else, road kill resurrected in dust

& the light of blue sky. I deserve
the chair for all the killing I've done,

but there was that day in Missoula
where you took the green you'd been

keeping & bought me a suit all paisley
& pink & used the rest on a dress

that made you bloom & twirl without
my helping. You took my hand & we pretended

we weren't running. We waltzed our time,
whistle-cooled diner coffee on my dime,

told the waitress we were married
& expecting. Nothing is realer than

an honest lie. & nothing's more fun.
God's a good lie. & even God knows –

you can chew fat & still stay thin
& love is both a blessing & a sin.

# LITANY OF WHAT WE KILLED

Three dozen flies swatted to guts
on the glass weapon of our windshield. Two
signposts felled like trees into the dust
by the county road. Buckets of beer
I cannot count. An ashtray of cigarettes
& another & another. Our faces under headlines
of each local paper - we killed ourselves
in flame, used the flame to start a fire
once in brush & bramble & then we ran away.
A rabbit I butchered with a shotgun
so I might have a lucky foot. A hotel
door we kicked in while making love
rougher than a chainsaw. Your dress
whipped out the window & into a sky
full of the dust our wheels kicked up
when you said you wanted to ride
topless & free. They will say people.

They will read names & other people
will get sad. They will not say flies or rabbit
feet. We are all going to die anyway,
each faster than another. Stranger or not,
the moon shines a serpent beam of light
through a hole in the sky. This earth
is wild & man is made of its minerals.
What does that say about all this living?
They will say criminals & refuse to call us
lovers. But we did not kill our love. We did not
kill our love. We did not kill our love. When
they wanted us to die, we tried to catch
raindrops on our tongues. We danced barefoot
until the road was not a road but a song
& everyone was moving too fast
to catch a glimpse of who we were.

# WHY WOMEN MAKE THE BEST KIND OF KILLERS

*Today's the kind of sky that is no color,*
*it's got too much sun burning through,* he says,
& she goes rummaging, then comes,
can of paint in hand they used
to turn their car a different shade.

I tell this knowing you can't
brush a cloud atop the universe. I tell this
knowing you can't stop a thing from happening
that would happen to you anyway.

*There's laws you follow,* she says,
*cause there ain't no better choice. Everything else is just what*
*you break along the way.*

She takes the brush & blues up

her own hands, & then a sky above her rouge,
an ocean upon her eyelids.

I've seen this, I know,
in other places, the things
one can do to play a different game
with nature. Once, I saw my grandmother
turn her own eyes inward
as she was dying to look her killer
in the face. She mumbled in tongues
& I believed the spirit who rules
whatever we choose to be
glistened gilded in sweat
like the sun's watered reflection
against her skin.

                    When she died, then,
I knew it was only because
she was tired of defeating everything
that had once tried to kill her.

In the car, the man sits —
a statue crumbled in the aftermath
of war. The woman strips
wild & bare & blue
& goes running with a shotgun
pointed toward the sky.

The next day, the papers reported
a dozen shooting stars. You know

there were wishes too.
It does not matter what's real
or what is simply the gleaming leftover
of another's attempt to escape
what they cannot ever leave. Most men
I've known have spent too long
feeling stupid & sorry for themselves.

I know, I know:

life is short some days
& some days it is long. You tell yourself
it will be ok until it's not
& even then, you persevere. It was
women who taught me this.

# THE STORY OF HOW YOU & YOUR BROTHER GREW UP

You are Irish twins, born somewhere between a year and two apart. You share the same room for an infinity, his bunk on top of yours. You wake up early, rip into a package of Oreos while the cartoons dance across the screen. *You* refers to you. *You* refers to both of you. You watch him grow into his leanness. You wonder if he remembers the night you woke up in the house alone, the two of you, a storm highlighting its jag, zig-zagging through the haze of purple clouds, how you both laced up Chuck Taylors green as seawater, and ran to the neighbor's. You know early on it was always about running. You play high-and-seek with the whole neighborhood. You sneak through the alleyways, stash yourself in trashcans. You share dreams without speaking them. You learn to talk without talking, hours in the basement, ignoring the call for dinner.

# BROTHERS IN TOWN

Father never let us go out much
so we learned to play together.
Two of everything — animals
in the belly of the ark Noah built
lobbing baseballs through the cold.
I don't know how, but blood
stays warm. Some nights I wanted
to push my finger through your body
like a child damming up a wall
to keep you from flooding out.
I don't want to lose anything —
there was that time I overthrew
your running hands & had to watch
as you dodged a car to save
what I had tossed. It didn't work.
It popped & air came spilling out
& I laced my fingers atop my head &
cried. Father gave you his old Ford

when you aged faster than me
& I was scared you'd drive away.
You always came back. They say
blood knows blood, but I know
it never leaves the body that keeps it
unless some kind of violence
disrupts its flow. I am obsessed
with all of this, how I can bring
my eyes to tears just by thinking
of your leanness humming
through a night so quiet we had
to soften our footfall. We were
playing hide & seek, just the two
of us, just like we were used to.
I think that's what I mean
when I talk about life. Those nights
I watched the neighbors dim
their lights one-by-one & worried
I would lose you in the dark.

# HIGHWAY PATROLMAN

You drive all night through stations
on the radio. Never mind
how some fog of music
could make you feel lonely, or the long
elliptical cables invisible at night, connecting
one house to another, yellow
like stars caught inside bottles
floating long a river. It's what you think of
that kills. It's the missing, the double meaning:
there's something out there
you don't have inside,
& there's nothing out there you do.
When the shortwave sizzles,
hisses at your loneliness, you think
it'll be someone other than the same voice.
There's a wreck fifty miles east.

There's a man bleeding in a pale circle of light
just outside a storefront. There's a shot fired
that could echo across the silence
to you. It's a silence that holds so much
you must feel eternal. Not in the sense
that you'll never die, no, just in the sense
that if you did, no one would know
until sunlight. You got it, you say,
but it'll take time. The smoke will clear
the wreckage & the blood
will harden like the yolk of an egg.
If you want love tonight, it'll have to wait —
most good things do.

## WATCHING YOUR FATHER DRIVE

As your father loads a cooler of Diet Cokes
into the trunk, you slink in back, sweater
as a pillow, the night's cemetery marble-lit

by the headstones of stars, each one
a dead thing you will never meet
unless what they say about death is true –

that people linger up there to watch. You think about
this often, how your dead aunt Patti
might be sitting in a chair someone fashioned

for her somewhere in the heavens, looking
down, eyes wide despite the dust
of universe, never growing tired. You

want to sleep but never do. Instead,

you follow the yellow line's blur
as your father tunes between Springsteen

& The Band, as Rick Danko sings *it makes
no difference how far I go, like a scar the hurt
will always show.* If you could find sleep

that is not steeped in nightmare, a sleep
as restful as the dead, something that does not
make you toss the sheets aside, if you could

just put off aging for a little while & stay
forever young, you think you might have
a better time at all this living. Nothing exists

but time & what it does to you, how you
can't help but notice the melanoma
spotting up your father's hands, how he

sometimes has to wear gloves to keep
the sun from killing him. Forget about
all of that & try to imagine a life

without the need to be by his side.
You have his handprint decorating
the thin room of your skin. It makes you feel

like you must pay something back. You stop
at a gas station on the other side of a river
someone famous must've crossed. You let him

buy you & your brother hot dogs & Cokes.
You ache years later when he is not around.
When he dies, you will believe in whatever

false knowing might keep him around
for just a little while longer. Please, never
grow tired of traveling. Time is better spent

narrowing the space between what you love
& where you are. Each day prays a rosary to this.
You sit in the backseat of your father's car.

You lean your head against the steam fogged up
into a kind of pond upon the glass. You eat
your hot dog & listen to your father's music.

You watch him drive near-asleep through
a night so long it must be someone else's life.
You are so much his you cannot contain

your love. It will pour out of you into
a stranger who will never understand. Kiss
him for me when he is done, & take over.

# ELEGY FOR MARIA & MY BROTHER

It must be hard to love two brothers
& feel the fingers of each graze
first your near-silk of dress & then
the translucent hairs atop your arm
as you twirl in circles underneath
the hanging lights of an old barn.
You took off your heels, watched Franky
sip whiskey till he teetered toward
a different rhythm, but still remained
his brother's brother. Sometimes I
miss my bear my blood my brother
of muck & mud, & wish I could kiss
the salt crystal'd on his eyelashes after
a long run through the night, or dance
among the jewels of fireflies until
we left with different lovers. But he
always came back. Franky didn't —

Franky, who kissed you once
with lips as chapped as wallpaper
before Joe took your hand & ringed it
with wire. Somewhere, there's a night
as quiet as sleeping cattle, a dark
that rises & falls like a breath heaved
out of lungs charred dark with Marlboros.
It's not this one. This one flickers violent.
Maria, your dress is redder than the end
of the cigarette you let rest between
your lips while you wait for Joe
to let his brother go. They're chasing
each other past the county line, under
the light of stars & sirens, out toward
Canada, & they're leaving you behind.
It must be hard to love two brothers.
Sometimes, I stand in the never ceasing
noise of the dark I know & remember
how my brother's thumb was the size
of a clementine. So nubbed & large
& ripe, I could hold it forever.

## MY FATHER'S HOUSE

I have no stories to tell. Once, I stared
                              at the
word *love* until it became
*leave*
     & dreamed a night that rose from ground

once daylight left.

My father most days came home late, hands
      greasing a bag of food.
                              We gathered round
the television
until the food became the nothing of the air
                                        we
breathed.
You can play a memory
                    through the caught lines of
your mind
until it becomes a dream

         you don't believe in
anymore.

You can do this with your whole life. Time happens
     at the same pace no matter what

you fill it with.

Some days my father wears gloves to keep the sun

from killing him. We joke about death
often.
    He says
       *what will you do when I'm gone.*
    He says
       *oh how you will rejoice*
           & I say *yes,*
*dad, yes* because I know
this gentle lightness eases the pain of life,
            the
slow ebb & flow of forever
   my lover worries too much about.

My father was my first lover.
        He taught me the
kind of touch
that never wakes another, so gentle
          it becomes a
kind of breeze

     softening their dreams.
When he breathes
    at night, violets bloom from his
dead mother's chest.

He does not know this,

                how he taught me to believe
                                    in his divinity, how
            prayer is only
                        another word for singing
                                        the gospel
                                                    into
            your parent's silent mouth,
            how *father* holds the same meaning as *author*
                                                    & we
            are all living in the novels
            others have created.

                            See, how in all this
            piecing together
                        of my father's house,
                                        this tender
            mortar of memories & words,
            I am only left
                        with fragments.

                            Sometimes, I arrive home
            late,

            a journey softened by warm beer
            & the rocking roll of an old train.
                                        When the crowd
            of strangers

                        disperses,
            my father arrives, shorter than the rest,
                                                    & stout,
            & shoulders my bag.
                            I say *no* & he reaches a hand
            paled
                        by the violence of sun that comes

                                                after
burning,

lifts the strap from my body
        like a man still so used to holding
a child,
        & carries this part of me
                        all the way home.

# THE STORY OF HOW YOU & YOUR BROTHER GREW UP

You go fishing with your mother's new husband. There's a picture your mother has – the two of you, one's pale skin slathered in sunscreen, and yours – tan, like your father's mother. You remember the tightening of the line, the cut of it through the water, the way any object you hold can become a knife, and how your brother yelped, how he snagged the fish out of water, much smaller than either of you had imagined. You label these years later as a litany of fragments. You try to piece together what really happened, the way memory can become a knife chopping up the order of your history, the whole narrative of what made you who you are. You often forget that your brother was there the entire story. Eyes wide. The sun's cruel violence dappling his paleness, setting him on fire.

# OPEN ALL NIGHT

At the Flying J
I sneak a piss between
two truckers heaving
some kind & oiled exhaust
out their lungs. Most days
my dick sways limp,
hanging dangling
like the rubber of a hose
you'd feed a baby through if that
was the only thing you had.
How ugly, power is.
Most men I see
I never talk to.
What would I say
anyway. *Hello, my stomach*
*sometimes aches a heaviness*
*& most days I feel like no one*
*wants to hear my language.*
I buy a bag of peanuts, a t-shirt
adorned with wolves
that I will never wear. 24 hours

is a long time to be open,
let alone live a life.
If I narrated my days
you would say
*get the fuck over it,*
*die faster already.*
Outside, New Jersey
is the gessoed canvas
the trucker paints
with the ember fan
of his cigarette —
*star light, star bright*
*someone's gonna die tonight.*
Bob Ross would find
nothing happy here.
I try to understand
killing. If I strain my ears
I can hear all the cats
that ran away. They're
plotting some revenge, scheming
lines that might divine
a new religion. I'm the sway
of a bridge you never see.
I'm so invisible
I get scared I'm pissing
out my soul. 24 hours.
Some people live here.
The highway is over there.
You can hear the sound
easy. That moaning drone

of a million people
driving all at once
& then being replaced
by other people driving.

# ATLANTIC CITY

I figure hope has a place & hope
has a time. I figure some nights
when I'm not warming up your bed

you don't take too kindly to my ghost,
the way he does not hum or murmur
or pull you close because he needs you.

My friend's obsessed with the way
the mob can make a body not exist.
There's a forest with sand as soil

somewhere in New Jersey & I hear
there's no mark a shovel leaves –
cut of metal through erosion, earth

giving way to man, then hiding him.
I don't know what I'm saying anymore.
Most words don't matter unless

they can resurrect the dead, & I don't
think this has happened before. I know
Jesus said *come out* & Lazarus did

but only John bled the ink to tell
that story, the other three thinking
it wasn't either necessary or true —

if you know the answer, keep your mouth
shut. I have a guilty pleasure of relishing
in mystery. Like how it's been days

since the sunrise unwound its orange
spool of thread between our bodies
in your bed & how I do not know

what it must be like for you to be naked
while I close my eyes & how I have no idea
with what tenderness or awkward, just-

waking lack of dexterity you dress yourself
as I sleep through your coming-to-know
the day. But if you bent the ten freckles

that loiter below your lower lip & whispered
*come out* just before you left, I'd spend

the day draped in your velvet

walking between the shadows for you.
I meant to invite you to Atlantic City,
to quell some anxiety by gambling & pretend

we're richer than we are, long skirt lifted
by the breeze of whiskey, a cigarette
I twirl too close to your hair – your fingers

gripping me like the handle of a slot machine,
brush of skin on steel, an equation of flame
& the ruin of a bed it leaves behind,

but a poem is a kind of gamble & language
has no truth other than its taut & curved
existence & when I say I love you

doesn't that scare you just a little?
I could bite my tongue, but everything dies
& some days I still believe in God.

# FRANKY DRIVES NORTH ON 385 TOWARD CHADRON

They say there used to be gold here,
& you hear talk of how it used to travel –
the freight slow-rolling north toward Custer
& Deadwood, the gold drilled from hills
blacker than granite cloaked in the shadow
of midnight, then the load-up, the long road
back from Dakota to Nebraska. They say gold,
but all I see is the play of sun on rust,
old Chevy's stacked into a Stonehenge
made of rusted metal & the whims of old men.
The world could be bad
or the world could be good
but tell me if that matters at all –
think of the way skin burns under sky
until a man can wear the flame he wishes to be
inside & how that thin organ

draws taut around the bone of face & fingertip
like music & how, after making love,
a man can sink slow into that crook between
her neck & collarbone & feel himself softening
but not have the urge to leave. There is a need
that is alright to admit & alright to have.
It is as valuable as gold, as pretty under starlight.
It is a voice I had never heard before
& the way it felt so familiar, like my mother's.
There is a sound a wheel makes
as it turns along a road. It goes *hum*

like the song of a wetted finger spinning
round a rim of glass. They say
there used to be gold here.
See the sun tricking the senses. I am a fool
for all this love & want & the way
sometimes the morning wakes into me
before I open my eyes, & how, when I do,
all this light comes blinding out. Bad men
came long this road wanting to be rich.
Most men are bad, but even bad men need a path
to travel. There are a lot of roads in this country.
Some moan low notes toward the heavens
as they curl like sheepdogs under sky. Ask me
for a fool & I will give you my hand. Beg me
for gold & I will give you a kiss.

## AUBADE FOR A NEBRASKA MORNING

Let it be new skin suturing a wound.
      The final drops of blood washed
off a body in the shower. The water

in the drain, the drain itself. Let it be
      what you said to me once.
We were naked & morning sat simple

& growing like a child between us.
      You didn't want to leave the bed.
Let it be that. Let it be simple

& kind. I know love isn't & I know, too,
      that patience most often yields
no rewards. Let it be dust gathered

in your palms, a hand closing, & then
        the dust turning to coffee grounds.
Let it be steeped & warm. You don't

speak much about your troubles.
        I have to read your eyes
& in them sits a width I could build

a bridge across. Let it be the bridge.
        Let it be the river below.
Let it be the mirror you stare into

before pinning up your hair. Let it be
        in whatever spirit spurs the pup
to huff at the fog gathered rumpled

upon the bedspread of the land.
        Let it be not forgotten, the way
most forget the killing done here,

how the earth holds more blood
        than oil. Let it be how much I love
& how much I love you. Let it sit here

all day & never grow old.
        How I wish that could be true.
Look out the window by your bed.

See how the glimmer glitters
        up the grass. See how there's a path

& how there's no path at all.

Let it be whatever you make of it.
    Night comes & then there's a wound.
Let it be the crawling out, the healing.

# THE STORY OF HOW YOU & YOUR BROTHER GREW UP

You throw baseballs almost every afternoon. You walk to the field, start close enough to reach your fingers toward the other, touch. Each throw, you stand still and he steps back, creating a space wider and wider to arc the ball between. You don't talk. You don't understand until later how this can become a metaphor, the space forever-widening, the silence forever-silencing, the ball at first traveling the distance in a single, graceful twirl of orb through the sky, and then the struggle to traverse the gap, the ball one-hopping, the ball twice-hopping, the ball landing and then dribbling through the grass. You know now most things don't become a metaphor unless you make them one. You learn how easy that is, to un-say the real thing by supplanting it with something else. Something prettier. Something far less raw than silence, than loss, than your failure to step a little closer, bridge the gap with something other than words.

## WHY I MIGHT COACH THE LITTLE LEAGUE TEAM

*after Denis Johnson*

Outside I smoke a cigarette
while a plane's ambivalence
drones suspended like a cello
& some man screams at the television
lighting blue his windowpane.
There's so much nothing here
& I want to believe in all of it,
like how my high school girlfriend
cornered me at a party near ten years
after we ended & said I *want you to know*
*we had a good run.* But we didn't.
I remember nothing but my fingers
twitching the memorized numbers
in the longing for someone to talk to
because I didn't know then
that silence could be a kind of conversation.

I would go back now, though,
live in the nervous fidget
before I said *I like you* & kissed her braces
with my upper lip & bled all over her teeth.
Go back even more, pause before
my brother pitched the curveball
Alex Spiliotes hammered over the fence
& remember his eyes,
white against the licorice sky,
how they could've held the whole of everything.
A boy can know something for sure
but never give it a name, the softness
of not using a tongue to kiss
or of a ball drifting further from your hand
& over your head, & the fence, & forever —
where it still exists in a kind of night
like this one, where nothing happens.
I called the pitch & thought for too long I ruined
my brother's life. He stopped
smiling & even the light never dappled
the slight shoeshine of his lashes.
But our mother had just left us
& my brother was scared & there were fathers
launching themselves up
from their chairs like the cannon fire
of another generation to cheer on someone other
than my father's son
& Kristoph & Porter & Stephen
spun gazing as the ball twirled over the fence
& into the stars & I remember everyone's names

like a litany of the saints but none of this
is any good to me now. The next morning
brother & I took gloves & bubblegum outside
& I remember him throwing & me
talking like I had never talked before.
*Put it there, Tom. Nice pitch. You're throwing
faster than ever.* He either was
or he wasn't, but tell me
if that matters now.

# GOLDEN SHOVEL FROM ATLANTIC CITY

*"Everything dies baby that's a fact, but maybe everything that dies someday comes back"*
         - Bruce Springsteen, "Atlantic City"

I know fiction don't pay – I've heard everything
before, the dream-catch of lies, how a lover dies
just when you wake to honesty. You know baby,
I should stop calling you baby. I know that's
not hard. I love light, the way it dapple-shines a
night into tulips. I love a mess of sheets, the fact
of you morning in my bed. I'm old as age, but
come flying, I find the window, thinking maybe
when a house gets small, it'll stay. Everything

burns me to simmering & I'm missing you. That is no apology. You can run until your heart dies, but that don't mean your love will. Someday I'll die too. Here's my testament: What comes comes crying, but I get too sad to turn my back.

# FRANKY LINGERS AT A ROY RODGERS

I got it. Chicken is chicken.
*Cluck, cluck, fuck*
& I knew a woman
who wouldn't come
unless I moaned a sonata
between her legs. Come
to think of it, she might've meant
Sinatra. That's what
I'm thinking of when I rip fried skin
from breast & eat it
on its own, savoring
the seasoning that could be
road salt brined in oil grease.
I don't know where I am
& this is one of those moments
when I want to have a realization.

Press thumb to temple.
Chew down.
Hello God. I know
it doesn't work that way,
but I don't know
a sonata from a bushel
of flowers meant to look
pretty & if you gave me flowers
I wouldn't know their names.
I'd just smell them till they died.
Most things don't come
when you want them to –
a woman, a pup, a desire
to be a better person. This is
no excuse to say
I could've been a good man.
I think it makes me worse,
this knowing
that life is hard & I've
given in to leaving home
& eating chicken sandwiches.

# MAHWAH ASSEMBLY

I heard you bought a gun on account
of the apocalypse, twirled it round
drunk on gin & wine outside the club
the night they shut down the assembly line.
I know most men can't see past the next
roll of hill, twirl of leaf spinning in wind
left by a highway tire tracking through the miles,
& I know you didn't plan to shoot nobody
other than yourself, but the way your beard
looked like you had skinned it off a mutt
& how nothing good happens in New Jersey
except when someone can leave to sing
about it…well, you know, I understand.
They donated that plant's first car
to the local hospital. Can you imagine
if it came to take you away, your sunken

creek bed of a chest hollowed through
with fabric & wound, as if someone
had tried to skip a rock & failed? There's
nothing to excuse anymore, nothing
to condone. A body is a body until
it's a building & a building is a building
until it loses its purpose. Then it's an eyesore,
a wreck of stone & sediment filled
with the sad twist of tired trees. Now,
you can ride up the bronchial ache
of Stag Hill Road & find a group of natives
boarding up their homes, playing ball
on a field with no lines, just dirt & the kind
of dirt that used to be grass. It could've
been you, but once you become a man
you don't get away with being a child
no more. It's the way the world works –
you used to be wrenching a tire to a body,
& now you've got a son you'll never see
rolling the rubber of old Fords down
a hill after setting them aflame. It smells
so bad – the stink men leave trying
to cover up their sadness. That night
they closed down the plant, I could've
stopped you, could've sat you down
at my table & given you a knife & fork
& watched you cut through chicken
with the calm patience of someone
who doesn't participate in killing.
We could've talked sports we didn't

know & put off thinking of the future
for a little while. But all things come
back. You do what you do & you pay
a price. It's different for each man.
It smells like fire & rubber & alcohol.
It smells like birdsong & lilacs growing
next to asphalt. It smells like New Jersey.

# CONFESSION

When they found me there was so much
I tried to say. I wanted to tell a story -
how my life was more like anyone else's
than my own, but I knew I had grown
further earth than man, blood-soaked
& hiding, only a small feather of soul
peeking out of ground. I pulled a potato
out a hole in Idaho & replaced the space
it needed with my body. I'll die soon enough
& people will pray for my damnation. One
or two will bend for my salvation, knowing
an eternity is a long time to stay a bad man.
The others will know not to care. I had a friend
who doesn't know me anymore, but I
remember what she said. That people
do not change. I thought of this once
while watching someone else's blood

pool a circle so dark I thought I might
jump into it & disappear. I could say
so much. I could say that life is one long
confession for being alive & forgiveness
a kind of salve. I could say joy & sorrow
are the same feeling heightened in two
different directions & that there is nothing
to ease both your pain & mine at once.
Someone has to go. It must always come
to this. We take to avoid being taken
& seek an end to what disturbs us. I just
went about it wrong. Maybe you're born
with sense & then you bury it when you see
where sense gets you. When they found me
they thought I was so dangerous that they
gave me space. They gave me so much
of it. In between us, things grew & I
couldn't tell the water in my eyes from rain.
It was funny, what still needed growing.
I'm not trying to make light
of killing. There's just so much of it.
They walked slow toward me
like travelers pausing before a cracked
diamond of lightning in the sky. They said
nothing in screams that a whisper couldn't
have delivered. When they touched my hands
they said they expected them bigger. I am
just like you, I said. Everything is different
until I see it & then it is different still.

# THE STORY OF HOW YOU & YOUR BROTHER GREW UP

You sit in meetings underground. You recite the 12 Steps like a mantra, learn them backwards and forwards, find yourself repeating them in your head as you avoid the cracks in the sidewalks of the city. You learn to love this. The smell of books in the basement, the gathering of people you only see on Wednesdays, how you will only know them here, in this setting. How you only know their sorrow, not what they look like when they eat a cheeseburger and let the juice of its near-rawness bloody up their chins. But your brother, you know this about him. You enter the room together and leave the room together, one beside the other, the two of you inhabiting a both-ness you do not think will ever become a one-and-the-other-ness. Yes, you know the word *other* lives in *brother*. You spend nights waiting for his breathing to become a breathing of sleep, a deepening, and then, from below, you let yourself slip into it too. If only you knew then what you know now – that life is so much about how you live after you lose. Too much, no. Just so.

# EVERY BODY IS SICK WITH THE FLU

People come & they go. No one
remembers a crazy person or even the small
little things that make up
a day. The way my girl dips a French fry
in her Coke, the way we check
the locks before sleeping,
while outside the big world spins
like someone else's daughter
on the lawn of all this ear-nibbling.
I don't want to be famous, I just want
to be known. This town can hold
a few hundred people but when my girl
sits atop my shoulders, we look pretty tall.
You see what I'm saying. It's madness
not to want everything there is. I've got
no reservations. Suffering, I know,

sits on a couch next to joy
& even sex can burn a mind to mush.
They'll remember me
for killing my lover's mama –
her stepfather & half sister too –
not for the way a cigarette between
my lips made James Dean
look like child's play. I got
all day. Chase me & her
between street signs & apple trees.
Crucify me on the cross of your
best intentions. Tell me you think
the world has more than a coin-flip-chance
at becoming a better place. I want
my death to mean something. Shuck
your corn & splinter your finger
on the floorboards. Build a little house
& build a smaller one
to keep your heart protected.
My girl taught me how to dance
so my big foot doesn't land on one of hers.
It's a pretty thing, to be alive.
Our bodies are full of the colors
we use to paint upon this world. Blood
sings the same song as sunset
& paints the same red I get
behind my eyes
when I'm making love & hungry.
They will burn me alive
in a chair that singes the rooms

of the heart like a forest fire
rummaging through a cabin
trying to find some good thing
to set aflame. I guess
when that happens it'll mean
I did something good
by dying. For someone else,
I mean. You know I'll miss
the kiss of salt & sugar
on my old lover's lips.

# HOW TO USE OLD SPARKY

Shave the scalp till it glistens in its paleness.

Shave the ankles round which the straps
        will hold, tight like a mother's hands
        gripping her child upside down.

Wet the sponge & ring it of water until
        it's perfect. You must be perfect
        here. Otherwise, it will hurt.

Place the sponge atop the baldness
        & imagine a mountain melting but
        do not see the mountain sitting there.

Place the electrode upon the sponge
    & fasten. There is so much fastening.

    Attach the next electrode to the mountain's leg.

The mountain must see all of this, until
    now. Now, unwrap the black fabric
    from your fingers & twist it round
    the mountain's eyes. The mountain
    is blind, as a mountain should be.
    Think of all a mountain should not see.

Withdraw your body from the room. Pretend
    you are the last human leaving. Tell
    yourself nothing good remains.

Pull the switch & watch the mountain jolt
    & wait for the mountain to relax.

Check the mountain's heart. You must get
    so close & listen so hard.

Repeat. Repeat even though the mountain
    bleeds through its skin, so shiny
    & glistening. Repeat even though
    the mountain whinnies like a horse.

Repeat even though the mountain
breaks its own limbs, tries to unearth
itself from this holy dirt where we
return someday sooner than we want.

Tell yourself the mountain is an animal. Say
   *no one is human but me.* Say it again
     & again, until you are a mountain,
   too, of sweet meditation & blood.

## FRANKY DRIVES THE TRANS-CANADA HIGHWAY & STOPS AT A DINER

When she said whaddyawant
I guess I figured they don't serve coffee
in Canada. I dunno why. Tea

seems more Canadian, less
of a commitment to anything that'll
get you more fucked than you are.

So, tea & a plateful of scrambled eggs
& I thought they'd bring me ketchup
in a jar. They didn't. It was Heinz

& I was scared, kept checking
my shoulder for my brother, half-wishing
he'd be there to cuff me back home

like a stray dog. But I know I'm
as good as forgotten, a cloud made blue again
by wind & sun. I know I can eat

slowly now, but I still wolf my grub
even when I'm not hungry. I've ruined
so much I don't wanna lose what's

right in front of me. I sat & asked
for coffee in my cup of tea & then added cream
& then drove for miles on the highway

that ran along one of the Great Lakes,
looking to my left as I swerved. Somewhere
across that made bed of water & feathers

fallen from the gulls was a house, I knew.
Joey might be there wondering
or he might not. I got so much

I'm still trying to figure out. Look
at the sky. It's so big & so full of color.
Imagine if it fell. Imagine if it hurt.

# ICE FISHING

Take the road by the water toward town
in winter, when the snow's as white as sand
& the ice slumbers toward the infinite, take
the road up the hill & do not get too close
to truckers – I've heard stories of the rubber
slipping off their tires quicker than a hat
once flew off my father's head in a parking lot.
Past the diner neighbored by a course
of mini golf where a priest once hid balls
in his black pockets to cheat me – drive past
that corner & into town. Get a round
of beers & slide into the house full of guitars
& sit on an old amp & watch an older man
strum away on a hollowed-out Gibson.
Some say bullets are what kill, hollow-pointed
& loaded into guns, & I figure you've seen
killing done, a deer teary-eyed & staring

off into the distance of its new forever
where no one has the time or place
for memories. But I'm talking about a boy
I know who owns a dog & how he can sit
on his couch plucking the top string
with his thumb & how the dog can watch
until she begins to sing. I'm talking about
how music is a kind of killing & how sometimes
killing isn't all that bad. If you drive back
the way you came, stop in the lots beside
the lake. You'll see a car there & wonder why.
Look out, like you didn't do before, & you'll
see a man looking like he's wandering
into a fog so cold it can freeze off your nose.
He's got time & a want for food. I've got
these things too. There's a lot we aren't
given. When I get sad, at night, near-sleeping
in my bed, I think of this. I don't want to.
I've got enough to give & enough to take away.

# AUBADE FOR A NEBRASKA NIGHT

Believe me, I know there's a wound.
    & believe, too, the definition
of everything. That night can be the sea

you open your window upon in dark.
    That sometimes there's nothing
to hold onto but your mind & even

your mind can be an anchor
    cut away from boat, drifting long
& deep to a ground where you'll

never set foot. Anything can be anything
    & that's the trouble with everything. You
want to find the line that separates

sky from ground, but when you lean
   out your small square of city,
town, it's dark & then darker shades of dark.

You could wander into space
   if you aren't careful. You could
mistake a lake's reflection for stars

& drown. You could fall off this flat earth
   that never seems to turn when you
want it to. That's the way it is

with wounds. They heal & then
   there's a scar, & if there's no scar, there's a
memory, which is forever

a kind of scar you can trace the finger
   of your mind along until
even the tangent of a tangent –

the echo of a boy's voice singing
   through the quiet, a car sputtering
before its start, smoke too far removed

from smoker – reminds you of where
   you've been & still how close
you are to the past. The night

is good for that. It lasts & then
   it lasts. Or it disappears

like a bullet through your eyes & waits,

purple-tongued, licking the edges
        of sky, to come back. I can understand
everything because of this. I see you

at your window in your longing
        for clarity. I see the world well up, cobalt, in
your eyes. You are an explosion

of searching. It will drive you crazy
        & your crazy will be beautiful
because it will contain so much.

See how your vision adjusts
        in dark to take in what little light
there is. Love's a scary game to play –

it has no shadow or color. It's a liquid
        you pour into a dark glass. Your mind
wants no part of it. I know this.

I have no advice for this.
        You sleep & then you wake up.
Life is funny because it has no metaphor

other than itself. By morning,
        you will find the edges of buildings
scraping an axe along the hollow

orange of sunrise. You will take a shower
        or you won't. You will hang your hair
to dry & forget to lock the door. It's

okay. You will go back. It doesn't
        matter anymore if you did or did
not. It's the going back that counts. It's

the way you brush the lone wet strand behind
        your ear, how rain is falling through
the steam of your coffee, how a child is singing.

# THE STORY OF HOW YOU & YOUR BROTHER GREW UP

You watch your brother run. You lose weight for the simple reason of being able to run alongside him. You learn that your brother speaks in new languages, that running is a language of breath and lightness, of rhythm and decision. You never become as fast as your brother, but you become fast enough to slip into his slipstream, to be the foot that falls in the divot his foot created for you. You learn this new language. You mimic your brother's tender footfall, his low hang of arms. You know now that there is a poetry of words and a poetry of place and a poetry of how you inhabit space. Your brother emerging from the dark shade between trees, chin high and hands by his waist – this is a kind of poetry. You say yes. You say you know most things cannot be changed. You say the world hums and turns and we can only move through it in the directions we choose at the paces we can manage. Your brother wakes every day to run between the trees. You know this, even hundreds of miles away, you know this.

# POEM FOR MY BROTHER RUNNING AROUND A TRACK

Let me begin with a question, how
to write a poem to a ghost, brother's white legs
burnt scab red & auburn, fleeing strangers
in circles. Sun caught green in the space
between the high school track, charred the grass
to brown. Color is a thing as fleeting
as a life. Above, the PA droned, said
*the concession stand is open now,*
& below, entombed & never named,
some soldiers Union dead
or Southern became dirt & bone, grain.
No one can escape being forgotten.
We were in Virginia, & I learned
how to read my brother's face,
the slow widening of his eyes,
the length of gait, that almost-second

when he was flying. I can love him forever
in that circle. He always came
back around, each time settling behind
a different body, arms sawed blue with veins.
The night before, we sat with father
over chili & Cokes, watching the latent glow
of the television at the bar, chewing over
the nothing of our conversation. A boy
can stay a boy for a long time,
amused by the quiet
of his mind & the gentleness
with which a body can grow. In the years since,
my brother has broken his bones
half a dozen times, if only by the impact
of a foot on rocky trail, asphalt paved
by the light of stars & electricity. But then,
under a noon so high even the cannon fire
of another generation still twirls up to reach it,
he was invincible, my father & I
watching him bide time over the mile
before twisting to the lead around the turn.
Brother, what we learned then I cannot
put words to, that a winner is simply one
who finds himself in the place of his beginning
before the rest of the field. You found your home
in a crowd, with a jersey that didn't fit you,
gunmetal on your feet. Our bodies
have changed since. They will change
for a very long time, in quiet,
regardless of whether

we speak of it or not. So let them grow.
A gap will form between our bones as wide
as space. In a dream, this distance can be
measured in feet & covered, forever, by them.

# MY FATHER & I AT A DENNY'S IN LANSING

When we woke & realized there was nothing
to do, we went to Denny's, sat each to a booth.

I ordered coffee that drank & refilled itself
& watched my father sip a Coke through a straw

while we ate eggs slowly, without speaking.
If I could tell you more, I would, but there was

still nothing but the ringing clink of fork on plate
& from the kitchen, a chatter above the hissing.

Younger, I read books that said things like:
*a man's eyes hold stories, you just have to look* –

but underneath the dewy film of eye is just

a cloud, & behind that, a nerve, & through that

travel signals of depth & light & color
& you can spend a lifetime looking at a man's

dilations & never know anything but how quiet
he keeps his own. I barely know my father well

enough to eulogize his passing, but the story
is not just in the silence of his eating. No. See us

at a Denny's in Lansing. See the way he holds
his fork tightly & slides one spear through yolk

so as not to lose too much too quickly & how
he cuts the white of egg into little squares

& moves them slowly toward his mouth.
Something must inform all of this. See how

I don't ask. It's what's here that's important –
how cheap the food is & how the coffee

keeps coming & how I could sit here forever
with my father. There's nothing out there

that concerns me. It's his slow & patient eating,
his fingers, his fork, his slight smile, his silence.

## FRANKY STOPS AT A PAYPHONE TO CALL HIS BROTHER JOEY

Rattle of coin
then voice, then
voice my own:
Joey? –
Yeah. No. –
This –
No, this –
This isn't,
I don't know
who Franky
is –
I'm just –
What's that –
I'm –
No, I don't
know a Franky –

I'm calling from,
wait, does it
matter?
I'm sorry
I must have
the wrong
number.
No –
Not that –
It's nothing.
I just don't know
how I knew
your name.

## UP ALL NIGHT

Fold up that Texaco roadmap
marked up with someone else's pen —
see another's line that sliced some states in two,
spanned a bridge across one of the Great Lakes
where there isn't one. I don't know much
beyond the roads my father
drove me long. I remember how he
never let a stranger pump his gas
& how once he drove for miles
while resting his eyes. Sometimes
we'd pass between that space
where one radio station tried to become
another & the songs bled into each other
not knowing we were listening. Do you
believe music can wrestle the silence
of a valley into a fog? Do you see us
rolling through it? I liked

to think of someone I would never meet
lifting their eyes through a window atop a hill
to witness the warm glow of blood
lighting up the road like a lantern
pulled along the vast gravity of this earth.
I'm sure it meant nothing, then, & still
doesn't. But it means something to me now
& doesn't that count for anything? Years later,
my ex-lover's car failed just after the crest
of a hill in West Virginia & we rolled
by the sheer grace of science
down & pulled into a gas station
while a woman soft-spoke into a microphone,
her voice traveling invisible through the night
& into our ears. People told their sad
stories & she responded with song.
We could've called in,
trembled our story along to her, become
two voices in the choir of sorrow
that is this world. But we sat still & tried
the car again & listened to it hum enough to start
& I have no permission to tell this story
or the story of my father driving all night
to see his mother or the story of anyone
I have ever loved or still do
but if you look at this map again
you will see with what hope some stranger
planned out a journey, dreaming
that a bridge would be built by the time
he reached a shore. You don't need me to say

it doesn't work like that. But tell me
what you would say
if I told you I believed it might.

## REASON TO BELIEVE

There is the sound
of strangers sleeping
in ones or twos,
separating in dreams
as the night metabolizes
the stars, eating them
with a wide open
mouth. Don't lie
& tell me a story
about the darkness
as something kind
& gentle. It's scary.
Sometimes it took
my father's belly
for me to fall
& when I did,
I dreamed him

shattering black
with sledgehammer,
& light came
crawling back
through a hole
in the sky that I
called morning.
I need a you
to be talking to
for me to make
sense of it all.
If I knew how
to sing, I would be
in constant lullaby.
Instead I walk
the neighborhood
in the pull
of lulling, by
& by. The way
you can begin
one sleep together
& wake on other
ends of beds?
What do you
think of this?
Somehow, each
time I dreamed
upon my father's
gut, I found
morning in my own

bed. He carried me,
I know. He carried me
kind & gently.
Like a song,
you say. Like
the dark, you say.

# THE STORY OF HOW YOU & YOUR BROTHER GREW UP

You worry everyday that you have run away. You imagine a morning of waking, of slipping on your shoes, stripping shirtless in the sun, and taking off, north up Broadway to the George Washington Bridge, across it, and then south on 95 for miles, through refineries of New Jersey, over the Delaware Bridge, across the Susquehanna, into Baltimore and out of it and then into your home city, your mind silent as the 18-wheelers scream past with their large loads of nothing. To run back. To show up at doors you have left behind. You think what is all of this without mending? You want everyone to be alright. To admit what you have done. To call home. To say something more than I am sorry. To say hello, I am here, I am no longer gone, I am in the process of forever-returning. To slip the shoes off. To walk barefoot into the grass. To touch fingers across the gap. Yes, an *other* exists in brother. As in *one another*. As in one leg, then the other. Then the other. Then the other.

# NEBRASKA

If you know a quiet that sings
the song of footsteps, if you know
an open window is an invitation
to trespass on another home's
scent, if you know the lesson
of the Bible that says the man
who holds the taste of blood
in his mouth is the one who holds
the truth, if you know tall grass
from wheat, a cow's low & gentle
moan from the soft howl of a coyote,
if you know the stars & try
each night to count them, if you
know flank from shoulder blade,
when to rub dry & when
to slather with sauce, if you know

how to cherish your own shadow
& have already given it a name
& a soul, if you know your mother's
voice from a distance, if you know
the nothing that exists between
miles, if you know what your dreams
mean & if you keep a record of them
by your bed, if you know someone
just isn't coming back, if you've tried
& then given up, if you know one
song that keeps returning to your head,
if you sing it in the shower, if you
think someone is listening, if you
are sometimes scared of everything,
if you've been in love before, if you
read novels sprawled out in the backseat
of your parent's car, if some days
you prefer to watch the clouds,
if you feel alright alone, if you
want to meet someone who feels
alright alone with you.

# FRANKY'S APOLOGY

I remember when we was kids
Joey raced down the one hill in town
on cardboard taped to cardboard
& I'd follow, till our asses was rubbed
raw with snow & ice. We went till night,
streetlights blunt & blinding, just kids
fucking with the fact we was family
in a place where there weren't many names
to know. After, we sipped coffee
at the bar & slipped house whiskey in
when everyone was too blitzed to notice
or care, then leaned like tiny trees
stripped of leaves over the table & shot
& drank till the balls seemed to move
when they were sitting still. I know
later I stole cars & Joey let me go.
I know he stole my girl & I said nothing

but blessings at the ceremony. I wanted
nothing more than to stay a boy forever.
There's consequence that comes with
growing up, where the world turns & says
you got to suffer for the wrongs you done
& the wrongs done unto you. I've read
the good book, the word of God, & I figure
heaven's a bar dancing full of rum & wrong,
or it's an empty cathedral off to the side
of a snowy highway with standards too tall
for anyone to lay a living toward. I left
a trail of ash from cigarettes tilted out
of windows as I drove my contraband
toward Canada. I wanted to give Joey
some kind of path to follow in case
he got sick of always doing right. I'm nowhere
now, but even in nowhere I can still
see his baby face caught in the glow
of streetlight & snow as he slid aching
away from me. I never told him this,
how he looked something like a star
you would wish upon if you still believed
wishing would get you anywhere.
I'm wishing now, Joey. It's so dark here.

## AT THE END OF EVERY HARD-EARNED DAY

Last night in the glow
of an empty parking lot
I stood, the haze of water
hanging from a storm burnt
to orange, the night's plum
bitten open & left for flies.
I wanted to sit down, wet
my ass on pavement, feel
the purr of everything
buzz against my cheek,
& think of the way my father
sometimes stood for too long
in his underwear looking
at nothing but his own reflection.
When I believed in God
I used his name to stitch together
what I didn't know. Maybe
I'm wrong about everything –
that the murmur of electricity

singing through a wire singed
by the slow burn of time
is a kind of god. That the hush
of a cloud shying behind
the dark cloak of night just minutes
after crying is a kind of humanity.
You know that feeling too, don't
you? How you sometimes cry
without crying & how one day
you are struck by a desire
to go home, simply, & sit
by the window near your bed
& do nothing but hear yourself
breathe. You are alive, I know.
Here is the parking lot of your
existence. Notice how the empty
spaces puddle with rainwater,
butts of cigarettes little boats
that know no shore. Here is
the light hanging like dust
caught in another room you
remember now. Here is a memory
of your father in that room. Here
are his feet, the ample simplicity
of his body, how there are days
where you know nothing
but the longing to be held.
& who taught you that? That
the difference between want
& need is only how you make
up your mind. It's alright,
I want to say. To the lamp,
the throb of a car starting
somewhere, the scream
of someone screaming along
a song through the window

of a bar. I am not always kind.
There are days I give up. The night
thrums like silver dropped
from some great height. I once
held a baby to my face & kissed
her nose for the longest time.
To be wide & soft, to lay
your body down & feel
the gentle moan of everyone
ending their day atop you —
if you told me I could do this,
I would believe in anything.
When I was little, I held
an ear to my father's gut
just to hear him breathe.
I needed to know
there were others
somewhere in the midst
of all this dreaming.
Life is big & I don't know
what to do with it. If I have
to sit down, tell me
you will sit beside me.
We will eat each other
like plums. We will hum
a melody that never repeats
itself. We will put our ears
to our bellies, be still, listen
to the throb still throbbing.

# WHILE WAITING TO SEE BRUCE

After the tanker exploded, moving north on 95,
& the backup to the stadium stretched
for miles, I sat still in the backseat with Sean
& Vince, at seventeen, thinking how
my face would change if Springsteen played
I'm On Fire, or, something softer, that one
about the brothers off *Nebraska*, where

Joe Roberts chases Franky past the state line.
I do not have a shortwave, or a car to call
my own, only a brother who lives at home
with my father & works most days
& keeps softly to himself. The line
inched toward the potential sound, & soon
enough, we were still children, listening
for hours to a man far below. My brother
was not there, & he does not know
that sometimes, even now, I walk alone

& think of him, a runner, his chopped stride
turning around the tracks where we raced,
the final lap, chasing strangers down
the homestretch. I loved him then, those long
spring days under stretching sun, & I think now
I must have thought him some sort of angel,
gifted beyond belief. I should tell him this,
over the phone, or, years from now,
over beers, at a bar where we might meet,
both living on our own, or while our
grandchildren linger in a room beside the one
where we sit, our gap in age indifferent
to the years, Bruce still playing
on a radio, the song I wanted years ago,
having chased us down.

# MANSION ON THE HILL

To be honest, the house
        would be there
    whether you knew of it or not,
          a graveyard

with the echo of a ghost,
        some kind of haunting.
    You know the ritual
          of a small town funeral:

a body dies & each
        who remains pretends
    they knew him better
          & liked him better

than they ever did.
        They tell stories to summon

   the right kind of ghosts,
      & this goes on

& on. The procession
    of smoke that comes
   when candles are blown out
      one by one

into a kind of forever
     beyond where the last
  street ends & the first
      of some other life

begins. If you believe
    in the self as a funeral,
  if you wake into morning
     already mourning,

you know the heavy
    aching nothing
  of being alive. Children
     play in the yard

of a house no one
     has ever set foot inside.
  They tell stories to give
     themselves permission.

The house stands & always
    stands & watches

       & the children play
                & then grow old

& forget what it felt like
            to leave something
     behind. It's what
                you leave behind

that counts. When the slow
            train of cars
        rolls down the one
                road in town & then

beyond, past the last storefront
               with its halo of light
          rimming the smooth
                   glass of the infinite,

toward the mansion
               on the hill, who is looking
        to see what remains
                  in the yard? A bottlecap

from when we drank beers
            years ago
     & told stories of losing
                  our virginity,

like we were sacred.
              We were sacred

once. Never forget that.
                You get old

& you forget that.
        We were there, getting
    too drunk, telling
            ourselves stories

like we were loved,
        like we were heroes,
    like there was
            nothing stopping us

from becoming the myth
        of what we left
behind. We left
            that behind, too. We left

the yard, the creak
        of what listened,
    & grew up. Think
        of the self as nothing

but a dream. It's lucid.
        It's clear. It's a thimble
    full of holiness. It's so teetering
            & fragile it could

shatter when dropped upon cement.
        Think of everything

you've ever dropped before.
It's so much.

# NOTES

In "Litany of What We Killed," the lines that begin "They did not kill our love" owe a debt to lines from the far more necessary poem by Danez Smith, "Dinosaurs in the Hood," which, if you haven't read, I urge and beg you to read.

The Denis Johnson poem that "Why I Might Coach the Little League Team" refers to is the lovely "Why I Might Go to the Next Football Game."

The title of "Everybody Is Sick with the Flu" is based on the note Charlie Starkweather allegedly posted on the door of the Lincoln, Nebraska home in which he murdered Caril Ann Fugate's family.

"Old Sparky" is the nickname given to the electric chair in Nebraska. It is also a fairly common nickname given to electric chairs across the country, which I find beyond morally reprehensible — both the act of execution and the simple fact of giving a nickname given to a thing used to kill another.

"Golden Shovel from Atlantic City" employs a form invented by the great and beautiful Terrance Hayes. The form asks you to take a line or poem and use the end words of your lines so that the referred line or text or poem can be read vertically down the page.

Finally, many of the titles of the poems in this collection are borrowed from the titles of songs from Bruce Springsteen's *Nebraska*. They are, "Highway Patrolman," "Open All Night," "Atlantic City," "Reason to Believe," "Nebraska," and "Mansion on the Hill." The periodic emergence of Franky is an attempt to give voice to one of Springsteen's characters from "Highway Patrolman."

# ACKNOWLEDGMENTS

I am forever lucky that this list of thanks can go on for a long time.

Many thanks, first and foremost, to the great Bud Smith, who devoted so much of his time and care to this book. Books thrive thanks to the kindness and generosity of people like you.

Thanks also to my family and friends who are wells of endless support. Thanks to my father, my mother, my brother. Thanks to my ragtag group of strange writer friends. To my roommate Brian, and to Katie, George, Jared, Jeremiah, and the honorable, insufferably-angsty pup, Rosetta. All of you (even the pup) are inspirations through your own work and your own dedication and your own efforts. Thanks always to Meg, Ben, Johnny, Mel, and the so-many-more friends I've had and still have. Thanks even still to my teachers and to the numerous kindnesses passed down to me.

Thanks to the brilliant poets who offered to write some lovely words about this book – to Bianca, Joanna, Eduardo, and Bill.

And finally, thanks to Bruce, the Boss. I listened to this album many years ago for the first time and I still listen to it now. Certain things are timeless. They echo and they become touchstones for our lives. We are moved once by them and then moved again, in a different way, at a different time. Add this to the many reasons why we need art.

Devin Kelly is the author of the chapbook *This Cup of Absence* (Anchor & Plume), a collaboration with Melissa Smyth, as well as *In This Quiet Church of Night, I Say Amen* (ELJ Publications).

CPSIA information can be obtained
at www.ICGtesting.com
Printed in the USA
BVOW08s1011021216
469597BV00001BA/11/P